This book belongs to:

ISBN 0-7683-2050-X

D.L.TO: 460-1998

Text by Flavia and Lisa Weedn

Illustrations by Flavia Weedn

© Weedn Family Trust

www.flavia.com

Published in 1998 by Cedco Publishing Company

100 Pelican Way, San Rafael, California 94901

For a free catalog of other Cedco® products, please write

to the address above, or visit our website: www.cedco.com

Printed in Spain

The artwork for each picture is digitally mastered using acrylic on canvas.

BIRTHDAYS · ANNIVERSARIES

Celebrations of Life

A Book of Important Dates and Remembrances

Flavia and Lisa Weedn
Illustrated by Flavia Weedn

Cedco Publishing Company • San Rafael, California

*A*s we turn the pages of our lives,
let us be reminded that time is a
miracle woven with dreams, and we are *all connected*
in this **tapestry** of life. The greatest treasures
we hold are the **memories** of celebrations,
cherished moments of times shared,
and secret anniversaries of the heart.
Remember the dates of importance that matter
to you and your loved ones. Remember everything,
for sometimes it's the **simplest** joy
that can bring the heart its
greatest pleasure.

Flavia

Notes and Reminders

January

Just to be alive and part of the world is miracle enough.

Some people come into our lives, leave footprints on our hearts, and we are never, ever the same.

	Name	Occasion	Year

January 1

January 2

January 3

January 4

January 5

January 6

January 7

	Name	Occasion	Year

January
8

January
9

January
10

January
11

January
12

January
13

January
14

Believe in your heart that something wonderful is about to happen.

Name	Occasion	Year

January
15

January
16

January
17

January
18

January
19

January
20

January
21

Name	Occasion	Year

January
22

January
23

January
24

January
25

January
26/27

January
28/29

January
30/31

Notes and Reminders

February

Life's greatest celebrations

are anniversaries of the heart.

		Name	Occasion	Year

February 1

February 2

February 3

February 4

February 5

February 6

February 7

February
8

February
9

February
10

February
11

February
12

February
13

February
14

Each time I look at something I've loved, I realize the difference love makes to our hearts.

February
15

February
16

February
17

February
18

February
19

February
20

February
21

February
22

February
23

February
24

February
25

February
26

February
27

February
28/29

Blessed am I to have someone like you in my life, someone with whom I can share so much of me.

Notes and Reminders

March

When I think of all the things
that would have never been, if you had
never been, I celebrate the day
you were born.

Some people move our souls to dance. They make the sky more beautiful to gaze upon.

Name	Occasion	Year

March
1

March
2

March
3

March
4

March
5

March
6

March
7

Name	Occasion	Year

March
8

March
9

March
10

March
11

March
12

March
13

March
14

At quiet times, when there's just me, I think of all the gifts you've brought into my life.

Name	Occasion	Year

March
15

March
16

March
17

March
18

March
19

March
20

March
21

	Name	Occasion	Year

March
22

March
23

March
24

March
25

March
26/27

March
28/29

March
30/31

Notes and Reminders

April

We are each a part of all

that surrounds us.

Celebrate being alive.

Name   Occasion   Year

April
1

April
2

April
3

April
4

April
5

April
6

April
7

	Name	Occasion	Year

April 8

April 9

April 10

April 11

April 12

April 13

April 14

Lucky is this world to have you in it.

April
15

April
16

April
17

April
18

April
19

April
20

April
21

	Name	Occasion	Year

April
22

April
23

April
24

April
25

April
26

April
27/28

April
29/30

Birthdays celebrate the gift of time. Today we celebrate the gift of you.

Notes and Reminders

May

Our memories,

like our dreams,

are ours alone

and tell our story.

Be not forgetful to drink from life's cup, for life is brief and fragile. Do that which makes you happy.

Name	Occasion	Year

May
1

May
2

May
3

May
4

May
5

May
6

May
7

Name	Occasion	Year

May
8

May
9

May
10

May
11

May
12

May
13

May
14

A gathering of wishes that all your wishes come true.

Name	Occasion	Year

May
15

May
16

May
17

May
18

May
19

May
20

May
21

Name	Occasion	Year

May
22

May
23

May
24

May
25

May
26/27

May
28/29

May
30/31

Notes and Reminders

June

Life is a prize, an endless journey

of wonder and awakenings.

With each new dawn, let us

rejoice in the gift.

Name	Occasion	Year

June
1

June
2

June
3

June
4

June
5

June
6

June
7

June
8

June
9

June
10

June
11

June
12

June
13

June
14

They said all fairy tales must end. They never knew about us.

June
15

June
16

June
17

June
18

June
19

June
20

June
21

Name   Occasion   Year

June
22

June
23

June
24

June
25

June
26

June
27/28

June
29/30

Forever and always may the song in your heart be the song of love.

Notes and Reminders

July

If I could wrap love in a ribbon, it would be my gift to you.

Surely a star danced in heaven on the day you were born.

Name	Occasion	Year

July
1

July
2

July
3

July
4

July
5

July
6

July
7

	Name	Occasion	Year

July
8

July
9

July
10

July
11

July
12

July
13

July
14

Thank you for all the times you've made my heart sing.

	Name	Occasion	Year

July
15

July
16

July
17

July
18

July
19

July
20

July
21

Name	Occasion	Year

July
22

July
23

July
24

July
25

July
26/27

July
28/29

July
30/31

Notes and Reminders

August

May the child in your

heart stay forever.

Name　　　　　　　　　Occasion　　　　　　　Year

August
1

August
2

August
3

August
4

August
5

August
6

August
7

August
8

August
9

August
10

August
11

August
12

August
13

August
14

We are unaware of what sweet miracles may come.

August
15

August
16

August
17

August
18

August
19

August
20

August
21

	Name	Occasion	Year

August
22

August
23

August
24

August
25

August
26/27

August
28/29

August
30/31

Being close is an affair of the heart.

Notes and Reminders

September

Celebrate the gifts within you, on this day and always.

Life has treasures to offer, like love and beauty, and people like you.

	Name	Occasion	Year

September
1

September
2

September
3

September
4

September
5

September
6

September
7

Name	Occasion	Year

September
8

September
9

September
10

September
11

September
12

September
13

September
14

Follow your heart to a place where joy is shared and memories are free for the making.

Name	Occasion	Year

September
15

September
16

September
17

September
18

September
19

September
20

September
21

Name	Occasion	Year

September
22

September
23

September
24

September
25

September
26

September
27/28

September
29/30

Notes and Reminders

October

Sometimes it's the simplest joys that give the heart its sweetest pleasures.

Name   Occasion   Year

October
1

October
2

October
3

October
4

October
5

October
6

October
7

	Name	Occasion	Year

October 8

October 9

October 10

October 11

October 12

October 13

October 14

Each day brings its own gifts and sings its own songs.

Name	Occasion	Year

October 15

October 16

October 17

October 18

October 19

October 20

October 21

	Name	Occasion	Year

October
22

October
23

October
24

October
25

October
26/27

October
28/29

October
30/31

Birthdays are ordinary days sprinkled with stardust.

Notes and Reminders

November

Life is the music that dances through our days, our nights, and our years.

That which we dream of is born of the heart.

Name	Occasion	Year

November
1

November
2

November
3

November
4

November
5

November
6

November
7

Name	Occasion	Year

November
8

November
9

November
10

November
11

November
12

November
13

November
14

We share dreams, laughter, joy and tears, but mostly we share love.

	Name	Occasion	Year

November
15

November
16

November
17

November
18

November
19

November
20

November
21

	Name	Occasion	Year

November
22

November
23

November
24

November
25

November
26

November
27/28

November
29/30

Notes and Reminders

December

Heaven smiles softly and hears every wish.

Name   Occasion   Year

December
1

December
2

December
3

December
4

December
5

December
6

December
7

Name	Occasion	Year

December 8

December 9

December 10

December 11

December 12

December 13

December 14

Savor the warmth of family and friends, and give the most sacred gift there is to give . . . time.

Name	Occasion	Year

December
15

December
16

December
17

December
18

December
19

December
20

December
21

December
22

December
23

December
24

December
25

December
26/27

December
28/29

December
30/31

What a miracle of fate that we could live our lives at the same time on earth. How incredible God's plan.

Of Heaven and Earth

Aquarius
January 21 – February 19
Outgoing, individual, soulful

Pisces
February 20 – March 20
Artistic, sensitive, compassionate

Aries
March 21 – April 20
Bold, energetic, courageous

Taurus
April 21 – May 20
Loyal, determined, practical

Gemini
May 21 – June 21
Communicative, creative, visual

Cancer
June 22 – July 22
Emotional, home-loving, nurturing

Of Heaven and Earth

Leo
July 23 – August 22
Cheerful, powerful, proud

Virgo
August 23 – September 22
Refined, analytical, practical

Libra
September 23 – October 22
Companionable, pleasant, diplomatic

Scorpio
October 23 – November 22
Passionate, secretive, intense

Sagittarius
November 23 – December 23
Cheerful, generous, seeker of truth

Capricorn
December 23 – January 20
Ambitious, self-disciplined, moral

Birthstones and Flowers

Month	Gemstone	Qualities
January	Garnet	Consistency, perseverance, good health
February	Amethyst	Sincerity, security, peace of mind
March	Aquamarine	Beauty, honesty, loyalty
April	Diamond	Purity, invincibility, good fortune
May	Emerald	Faith, courage, foresight
June	Jade/Pearl	Tranquillity, innocence, longevity
July	Ruby	Success, devotion, integrity
August	Peridot/Moonstone	Fame, dignity, protection
September	Sapphire	Love, mercy, victory
October	Opal	Hope, happiness, truth
November	Topaz	Fidelity, providence, good luck
December	Tourmaline/Turquoise	Prosperity, piety, courage

Flower	Symbolic Meanings
Carnation	Bravery
Primrose	Youthfulness
Violet	Modesty
Daisy	Innocence
Lily of the Valley	Happiness
Rose	Beauty
Water Lily	Purity
Poppy	Peacefulness
Morning Glory	Contentment
Calendula	Introspection
Chrysanthemum	Truthfulness
Holly	Foresight

Some Old, Some New

Anniversary	Traditional Gift	Gemstone
1st	Paper, Plastic	Ruby
2nd	Cotton	Sapphire
3rd	Leather	Emerald
4th	Silk, Linen, Nylon	Pearl
5th	Wood	Diamond
6th	Iron	Jade
7th	Wool, Copper, Brass	Opal
8th	Bronze	Aquamarine
9th	Pottery, China, Glass	Spinel
10th	Tin, Aluminum	Ruby
11th	Steel	Amethyst

Anniversaries

Anniversary	Traditional Gift	Gemstone
12th	Linen, Silk	Peridot
13th	Lace	Topaz
14th	Ivory, Agate	Tourmaline
15th	Crystal, Glass	Sapphire
20th	China, Porcelain	Emerald
25th	Silver	Pearl
30th	Pearl	Diamond
35th	Coral	Jade
40th	Ruby	Garnet
45th	Sapphire	Tourmaline
50th	Gold	Diamond

Gift Ideas

Gift Ideas

Photo by Claudia Kunin

Flavia Weedn is one of America's leading contemporary inspirational writers and illustrators. Her work has touched the lives of millions for over three decades. Offering a kind of hope for the human spirit, Flavia portrays the basic excitement, simplicity and beauty she sees in the ordinary things of life. Lisa Weedn, Flavia's daughter and co-author, shares her mother's philosophy and passion. Their collaborative writings celebrate life and embrace meaningful core values. It is their wish to shine a beacon of hope into the lives of others by encouraging the belief that we all have a significant contribution to make in this lifetime and every dream can be realized. Their work includes numerous books, collections of fine stationery goods, giftware, and lifestyle products distributed worldwide. Flavia and Lisa live in Santa Barbara, California.